LOVE SURVIVES

AUTUMN RAE

AUTUMN INK PRESS

Copyright © 2023 by Autumn Rae
Published in the United States of America.

All rights reserved. No part of this book may be reproduced, transmitted, or distributed in any form or by any means, except for brief quotes used for the purpose of review, without the prior written permission of the author.

Any trademarks, service marks, or product names are the property of their respective owners and are used only for reference. This book is licensed for your personal use only, and may not be re-sold or given away. If you would like to share this book with another person, please purchase an additional copy for each person you share it with. Thank you for respecting the author's work.

Cover Designer: J Hunter Designs

ABOUT

For you who are grieving.
For you who are hurting.
For you who are missing something or someone that you used to have.
For you who are heartbroken.
For you who feel lost.
For you who desperately need to be found.
For you who need to heal.
For you who love and who need love.
These pages are for you.

For all the broken hearts who need healing

BREAKING

COMING UNDONE

Feeling scared that it's a habit,
love and leave, go on the run,
but never one to sit and settle,
you knew it was all coming undone.

WHERE DID YOU GO

I see traces of you everywhere,
little footprints, little hands.
I see your breath caught in the wind,
stuck in that cold November air.
And I stare – at your shadow – and I
ask, where did you go?
You were here long ago,
in this town with its trappings,
its collegiate happenings,
and with stale beer hanging lost in the air, I ask,
honey, where did you go?

I drive out to the end of the isle,
little waves lapping on the launch –
through a telescopic lens,
I see your dreams caught in a web,
dancing for at least they won't forget.
I see regrets rushing by,
haunting you like good-bye.
Your mind took over, wouldn't let you breathe,
wouldn't let you live life like you should,
you couldn't believe.

I smell smoke from your cigarettes,
choking off all those might-have-beens.
I see your life caught in a mess.

But I watch you take those baby steps,
and your wings grew
till you could take off your shoes,
your carefree life
snuffed out way too soon.

And I guess I want to say, before you've really gone away –
it was so beautiful knowing you,
and if the naked eye is true,
you'll be just fine and I'll stop crying,
for the you that I never knew.

Honey, where did you go?
It was so beautiful knowing you,
where did you go?

WELL AGAIN

All these bottles, pills and droppers,
sitting on our kitchen counter.
Fighting hard to beat your pain
feels in vain.
But you're the strongest soul I know,
always brave, ever fun, forever young.

I was wearing blue the day you fell down,
I threw the shirt away.
Laying on the guest bed,
you just wanted to feel free.
My heart broke when I saw you,
that I couldn't help you now,
but I vow...

You will be well again,
you will raise hell again.
I can't walk this earth
without you right by my side, my friend.
So you have to be well again.

You came home after a long battle,
hospital locks,
oxygen box,
all alone without a hand to hold.
But you were forever bold.
You won that war but felt the cold.
All my fears have been awakened,
your sad eyes, your little cries,
your heart is bruised but mine is broken,
because I don't know how to help you now.

Full of mischief, full of joy,
you'd chase your brother down the fence line.
You were always the best boy.
And I can't wait to see you do it all again
because I can't walk this earth
without you, friend.
So you have to be well again.

CAN'T CATCH YOU NOW

Walking a fine line between grief and numb,
hearing the agony in your voice.
Praying to save you, so silly, I know,
I could never reach you—
you were high as a star or
cold as the snow.

Can't catch you now,
blow me kisses as you soar away,
can't get you to stay,
you were here for the sun
but can't stand the rain.
Don't even stop for a bow,
I can't catch you now.

See your wings for the first time,
see how tired you are,
gave everything you had,
some was good, some was bad.
You were a hero even fighting mad.
I watch God's grace creep onto your face,
and I fall to my knees,
don't take him yet, please.

Raised me up on your broad shoulders,
tore me down when it grew colder,
helped me grow up when I fell down,
made me fight for every inch of my crown.
Right or wrong, you were effortlessly calculating,
desperately intoxicating,
fiery and filled with demons,
the kind of man who should go out swinging.

So don't you fall,
and don't you fly,
stick around
and don't say goodbye.

You were here for the sun
but not the rain.
And I can't catch you now.

BEND MY HEAD

I sit and read poetry to you.
You can't answer and I come unglued.
Geese fly by outside the picture window,
I absentmindedly wonder if there will be snow.
I don't remember the weather forecast for tonight,
but I'll never forget the look on your face
as your soul takes flight—
from your body—
tonight.

I bend my head and keep reading poetry to you.
But I've lost my place and have to start over.
I don't think I can get over—
you.
But I'll hold onto the memories.

I'm reading a poem about journeys,
you've already begun yours.
I put a photo of your late mother beside you.
I kiss the top of your head.
Not all wars are fairly lost and won.
Sometimes the devil destroys all that is good.
I raise my eyes from the page,
and I gaze—into your angelic face.
Violent no more,
soothed by the knowledge that you are almost freed.
But me...
my pain won't leave.
When you leave, the loneliness will engulf me.

I bend my head and keep reading to you.
But I've lost my place and have to start over,

I don't think I'll forget—
you.
But I'm remembering the memories.
And I'm smiling through my tears.
All the years
help me smile through my tears.

I WAS THERE

Death of a man,
a king among princes.
He put down his crown,
so he can rest now.

Worked to the bone,
he suffered alone.
I sat in the chair,
did you know I was there?

Your smile was the same,
you knew your own name,
the sun hid behind a cloud,
March days are so gloomy now.

Couldn't wait for the sunshine,
you were ready, ready to ride.
I rose from my chair,
blow a kiss,
say a prayer,
walk away,
and you disappear.
Like you were never really there.

Tears of pain,
hugs of grief,
I call out for relief.

Did you know I was there?

RAINDROPS ON MY HEART

You turned me inside out
and you flipped me upside down
as you taught me how to wrestle
on our grassy front lawn.
The moon was full and we chased raindrops together.

Whiskey from your glass tipped
onto my shell-shocked face,
and I laughed,
laughed with you.
All in flirty fun.

The rain kept falling and
the drops dripped down my shirt,
down my shirt and yours
as I pulled you in,
in,
into the messy puddle we'd made.
Raindrops on my heart.

When the clock chimed midnight
you ran onto the porch.
The rain was still falling on us, and you were
pulling me along but
pushing me away
as you stumbled on the porch step.

I tore myself in two on that uncovered porch,
my brain fought my heart, and the raindrops kept falling.
And we kept chasing them underneath the moon.

You touched your lips to mine, and

I felt the allure of sugared candy on your lips.

I couldn't trust your heart and you warned me that I shouldn't,
we weren't quite friends and we weren't quite lovers.

You were a danger sign I should have recognized.

But the raindrops kept falling on us, and you had already
captured my heart.
And try as I did, I could
never capture yours.
And long after we said good bye,
I could taste the sugared candy on my lips, and
I could feel the raindrops on my heart.

Years later,
when I saw you again,
it was another time,
another space,
and we were long over.
You had your arm around someone.
She had come along after me,
after you and I chased raindrops under the moon,
after our destiny had passed.
She had a little sugared candy on her lips.
The pain hit me because I knew I'd lost you for good.
I wished you well, and as I turned away,
the rain began to fall on me.
Raindrops on my heart.

THE GIRL WHO CARED

It was the beginning of time,
of our time;
I was growing up,
and you were too.

Your mirror
was a pedestal—
you put me there that summer,
and I stood upon it well,
so well, I could reach up
and touch a cloud with my fingertips.
You were the boy in the attic and I was the girl who cared.

THE ANGELS THEY CRIED

March was rainy.
I was crushed.
The news was expected
but I still wasn't prepared.
Darkness and grief,
wet stains on my cheeks.
Lottery lost,
and there is a cost.
You fought but you lost,
and we all felt the cost.

Merry no more,
you couldn't beat back the tide.
And the angels they cried.
The angels all cried.
I stared at my phone,

heartbroken and alone.

Disbelief at the news,
I prayed so hard for you,
But it didn't stop the rain,
couldn't slow down the ride,
and the angels they cried.

The angels all cried.

THERE WILL COME A DAY

She was lying awake after another bad date,
wondering what went wrong.
It had been a mistake
but she found out too late,
and that dinner went on forever.
His smile looked sincere,
turned out it wasn't real,
and she couldn't let him steal...
her heart.

There will come a day,
when you will not feel this pain,
pain that's driving you to tears.
There will come a day,
when these walls will fall away,
so get down on your knees and pray,
you can wash your tears away,
there will come a day.

FREEDOM RANG

Little secrets,
big, big laughs,
whispered to each other in class.

Got in trouble, got away,
we always dreamed we'd leave someday.

Best-laid plans
gone up in flames,
you wanted love,
I craved the fame.

You kept me grounded,
I kept you safe,
little girls,
just trying to find our way.

I saw your picture
splashed online,
looking so different,
when did life get so confused?

One day we're on the flying saucer,
giggling at the amusement rides,
the next we're fighting
over why it all came unglued.

Freedom she rang,

And time didn't stand still,
you stopped living for you,

all's was left was a chill
where you were.
I wished you well,
and time stood still.

RUNNING AWAY

You pick wildflowers in the dawn,
you speak to friendly ghosts when you're alone.
So many dreams gone up in flames,
all you've got left is your last name.
You dance freely when you're alone,
paint outside the lines in your own home,
fiery red hair shows off your eyes,
spitfire mixed with sass makes up your mind.

Running away,
you're always running away,
have to say yes someday,
but not yet—today you're still
running away.

Great big house you don't want,
prison walls filled with cement.
He speaks so quiet no one can hear,
you want to scream—in his ear—
make it clear—you don't want to stay here.
Saying goodbye to the contract made,
waving farewell to the dandelion wave.

He tried so hard to keep you still,
playing a role that wasn't yours to fill.
And your eyes gone dull begin to fill...
You say, 'lay me down, love me still,
paint my smile, break my will.
Peace gone mad, love gone bad,
break my smile, fake my will.'
And in the end, you'll fight to stay still.

Have to say yes someday,
but today you're going to keep
running away.

DO IT OVER

I held up my phone so I wouldn't miss a moment—
so I could capture forever in pictures all the love in the room.
Family and friends making amends,
you lying on your back, smiling like a brave soldier but wishing
your nightmare could be over.
Lump in my throat, my hands were cold,
my heart was breaking as I saw into your soul.

Pretty flowers in vases around your bedside,
they were vibrant and colorful with no hint you were ready
to die.
My newborn babies' pictures
surrounded you smiling and alive,
brutal contrast to the truth—
we were watching you die.

Do it over,
come back four leaf clover,
do it over again.
Stand up and live again,
wake up and be our friend,
do over and over again.

I flit around the room,
looking everywhere but at you,
your pain capsizes me,
can't bear to see you suffering.
You're too strong to go out like this,
too brave to fall down the well and
never recover like this.
Heroes don't die until they disappear.
Strong and brave, they walk away,

and I flit around the room before bowing to pray.

Take a breath,
let it out,
say a prayer,
I give thanks that you were here.

OLD FRIEND

I've been thinking about you,
is it sunny or is it gray?
I've been seeing blue skies these days...ignoring the rain.
Almost called you a million times,
then I put the phone away.
I hit the bars alone now,
laughing louder than I can think,
trying to outrace demons while I down another drink.

You always said I leave no stone unturned,
got no excuse except I hate bridges burned.
I miss your POV when my thoughts churn,
over and over in my head
while I lay awake in bed.

Been stalking you on social but you disappeared
so I made up a story of my own—
I see you with a baby who looks like you in a happy home.
Are you married, are you happy,
do you feel what's real each day,
or do you wash it all away?
We lived the crazy times together
but I've got no regrets.
Not caught up in playing life safe,
falling together was a fall from grace.

Yet here I go turning stones again,
and there you are hiding your true self again.
And here we stand at the same impasse we've always been:
there's me, there's you,
and there's what might have been,
old friend.

You were supposed to be my maid of honor,
we were supposed to teach each other's daughters—
how to be friends like us,
how to live, how to love,
how to pull each other up.
I wish you well, I wish you peace,
hope all our remember whens bring relief.
Small but mighty will leave a scar,
wound on my heart from reaching too far.
I won't ask where you are,
see you up high on a shooting star.

HEARTBREAK

Times are tough
but we'll be okay.
Times are tough,
but we'll make it.
Times seem hard right now,
but they'll get easier.
Our hearts may be heavy today
but they'll lighten up.
I know you never asked me for my love
I know you always pushed me off,
but I gave it anyway
and that's just the way it is.
I gave it all to you
and that's just what I did.
I lost you anyway, but
that's heartbreak for you.
I need to take my love back now
but I still have some for you.
I need to be on my own now
but I still have room for you.
I need you to be strong for you, okay,
and I'll be strong for me.
I need you to grow up now,
just like me.
I want to give you everything
but then I'd have nothing left to take.
I want to show you how to live
but that's not my choice to make.
I want to touch you endlessly
so you'll know how much you're loved.
But I will give you back your strength
by saying good-bye, by waving a hand,

by blowing a kiss, by saying—you can do it,
you can make it, you can cherish yourself
as you cherished us, and we can cherish ourselves
as we cherished you.
I love you, and I cut these ties, these balancing ties of woe.
I stand on my own, I stand on my feet but that doesn't mean
you should go.
Stay, and let the heartbreak go.

LIGHT OVER THE STOVE

Twinkling stars light up the sky,
feels like it's the fourth of July.
But we can't see it where we are,
our hearts are hurting with fresh scars.
An accident, an ambulance,
blaring sirens don't quit.
Playing telephone till everyone knows,
playing strong when
the thorns pricked the rose,
crying by the light over the stove.

It's safe where it's darker,
here hearts can talk louder
than awkward conversations in the hospital halls.
Come into the kitchen,
I'll give you a listen,
into what's going on inside my soul,
come sit with me by
the light over the stove.

Full moon on fire scorching white,
burning the embers of the night,
but we're holed away in our
own private pain,
huddled in blankets
unable to let go of today,
unwilling to put an end to
the news that shocked us awake.
When someone goes missing
we head to our kitchen,
searching for comfort and how...

nobody knows,
but we try
by the light over the stove.

YELLOW BIRD

You were my yellow bird,
how'd you win my heart?
Silly question,
because all it takes is time.
Time, devotion,
mission true;
to wake up in the morning,
his hand in mine,
to wake up in the morning,
with bacon frying.

The windows stayed open,
till the gales of laughter began.
You were afraid of the neighbors,
but not of my little girl.
You helped give her life,
a job so big,
a job dared by no other,
an unwrapped gift I hold forever.

My yellow bird,
flying to the sky,
will you look back and wave at me?
I think I could say good-bye.

COUNTING DANDELIONS

Counting dandelions together,
our hearts were made for forever,
you swore you wouldn't leave me here too soon.

I held you up so high,
I never took the time to cry
when you went away with no good-bye,
all you did was pick up your wings and fly.
I keep asking why.

And I'm left all alone
holding questions to the test
but with no answers,
you were the best
and now you've left.
And my life's a mess.

Why'd you come crashing down,
I needed you to play the clown,
disease isn't you, can't be true,
I knew you'd always stay,
somewhere, somehow, some way,
but you made me wrong
you're not allowed,
to go away,
so why, why didn't you stay?

I remember your letter
so carefully put together,
where you said that you'd get better and you promised
to see me soon.
I believed in that letter,

believed you meant forever
would never disappear like the moon.
I keep asking why.

Before November was spent,
I'd never see you again,
you went away so fast,
so soon.

Counting dandelions alone now,
I want you to come home now,
come,
come home.

ENDLESSLY

Pain laced with grief,
anger mixed with relief.

I felt your absence
like a door slamming closed.

I've never ever felt so exposed.
You protected me, walked
in front of me,
Sacrificed everything
so I could breathe free.
Never got to thank you
for all you did for me.

There wasn't enough time
for the ignorance of youth.
If I had one do-over
that would be my mulligan.
You held me up always,
let me into your heart.
Like life, we had time apart.
I hate our misunderstandings
and sour notes.
Wish the music was never bitter
and always sweet.

I love you endlessly,
send up hearts and prayers
relentlessly.

I wish we didn't have to part.

You protected me,
and I loved you endlessly.
You left me,
and I grieve you
for eternity.

BLOOMING

PICKET FENCES

White picket fences falling down,
falling down all around,
toppling like dominoes,
one on top of another,
on top of me.

Nothing to hold them up, to hold me up.
They stood around the yard for years,
protecting, soothing,
but eventually the ground beneath gave way;

that ground which had shouldered the burden for so long,
had been full of stones, stones large enough to be boulders,
and the boulders had strength but instability.

As time passed
and the pressure increased,
some of the boulders broke,
broke into one another,
and the explosion happened suddenly.
So the white picket fences could hold up no longer.
They collapsed, and with it everything I believed in fell with them.

As I stood in the yard, suitcase in my hand,
terror hit me.
The terror of starting over,
of being alone.
But in the middle of the terror,
a burst of emotion came through—
freedom.

WAS IT ME?

I love, and I hurt;
I feel, and I grieve,
I hug, and I wound,
I touch, and I bleed.

Was it my face?
Was it my laugh?
Was it too loud?
Were you too sad?
Did you not like my way
of being myself,
did you want me to be
somebody else?

You didn't teach me judgment.
The world teaches that.
But it also teaches acceptance
and self-love.
You couldn't give me that.
I am here, I am free,
I am breathing
so please step out of my way.
Let me be as I move forward
and say goodbye.

LOVE WILL REIGN

Broken and bruised and desperate to heal,
too easy to quit but I won't
end like this—stuck in a cave
with a big empty page.

Up all night long trying
to remember my song...

It's been too long
since I wrote my own song.

Let's fly away,
drive fast come what may.
Cowboys on the run,
trying to outrace the sun.

Working all day, no time to pray,
for the clues to the puzzle
can't even take time to cuddle.

Poison arrows all over,
need to find my four leaf clover,
honey break down our fence,
white picket was never us.

Losses leave holes too painful to close.
Sad and blue becomes terminal,
forget what it's like to feel normal.
Giving tree
spoke to me,
and she promised not to leave.
I write through the night,

if I get it all right maybe
then I won't fall apart if I sleep.
Feel the ache, let it pass,
gone too soon, gone too fast.
Walls creep up,
fear remains,
but love is eternal,
God is here,
have to trust love will reign.

ADDICTION

The end finally comes, let the party begin,
you reach for me and all you get is nothing.
My addiction came to an end,
and this is one girl who won't help you still.
I walked away before I could get caught,
caught in the cross-fire of you lighting me up
and watching me burn.

I SHOULD BE FLYING

I've been having a hard time at night,
so many unknowns in the air.
I stay up until dawn fighting demons,
don't want to keep using my sword but I've got no defense—
this is why I resist this.

I fell on the sand and the sand became the sea,
swam like a mermaid just trying to break free.
Now I'm staring at the screen praying it has the answers for me,
because we're all flawed with blood pumping in our veins,
and we're all scarred while we look for answers to anything.

But life goes fast and we shouldn't waste a day,
which is why I must forge ahead...

I should be flying,
get up off my knees and start trying,
there's a great big world to start climbing,
so I open my eyes
and start flying.

I aced all the tests but I still failed the course.
Too drunk on the drama to unravel my worst.
My secrets are buried in a box six feet down,
wishing all those who put them there
would start looking at themselves.
The answer's in the details,
the stars can still align—
the dust will settle and the chains will all unbind.
We'll stop walking the line.

Rooms of stacked boxes filled with old things,

bring in the cutters and clean it all up,
from old pain to old love.
We all should be flying.
It's a wonderful world we live in so let's
stand up and let our wings guide us.

TWO QUEENS

You—and me—we were both queens,
sharing a crown, nothing could bring us down.
We sailed past death and ran from hate,
wished on a shooting star, never gave up on fate.
When time stood still,
it was just you and me,
high on a hill.

Shooting our laser beams, rain from the sky,
no one could hear us scream, we were angels on high,
it was just you and me,
sitting on a cloud,
safe from the dragon fire,
we could inspire
two queens.

Fire,
we set the world on fire,
fire,
grow higher,
the lights don't burn out, they just light up higher,
filled to the hilt,
with the promise of freedom fire.

Your eyes were mine,
your words divine.
I spoke, you listened,
you choked, I saved you, every time, no questions asked,
couldn't sleep, too busy praying for you,
wounds too deep,
you didn't have a clue how to cure all that pain
running clean.

The magic of a renaissance,
the miracle of circumstance,
only you, only me, ride
till you're finally free.
Tell the truth,
keep the score.
You're the queen.
I'm the queen.

LAST MAN

When life feels all uphill,
do you think about me still?
When you're covered in dirt
and can barely stand,
do you miss me,
do you crave me,
white sundress and
my bare feet on the sand?

I thought we'd won
but I didn't see
the last hurrah from
those killer bees,
life's so quick
and I have regrets
and some I haven't
put down yet.

You were my all,
you were my hero
when I couldn't reach you
it hurt deep in my soul.
You were the one,
you were my last stand
and I still pray
you'll be my last man.

Do you still feel pain,
when the rain's too cold?
If it soaks your skin
do you look for a rainbow?
Do you ever cry

instead of acting tough,
I know this world
can mess you up.

I watch the stars
up in the sky,
I hope for peace
every night.
Our love was broken
but not our bond,
I'll always want you in the light, holding
your magic wand.

Sometimes I feel your lips on mine,
you were a gorgeous Valentine,
remember me like I was back then,
full of a life that will never end.

You were the one,
you were my last stand,
but I've stopped praying,
I've finally stopped praying,
that you'll be my last man.

I WAKE

I wake from my numbing slumber.
And I stand on my own two feet,
and look in the mirror at my reflection.
I am strong.
I am worthwhile.
I am ready to take on the world.

BLOOM

The cherry blossoms came out today.
Dainty and gorgeous and eye-catching.
I could still be bright on my own.
I could still bloom.

ALL

Your laughter and your gifts,
we took them all.
Your bossing and your silly lies,
we took them all.
Your silence and your demands,
we felt them all.
Your pity and your knowing looks,
we felt them all.
Your tears and your grieving,
we cried them all.
Your losses and your pains,
we cried them all.
Your essence and your love,
we loved them all.
Your life and your devotion,
we miss them all.
Your heart and your soul and your never-ending love,
I am grateful for it all.

MOON BEAM

I hold myself in check,
legs drawn up tight,
the full moon howls high above,
its brightness trying to light my way.
The rain bounces down, then up,
up from the sidewalk.
It is a lonely night in the city.

The streets below my window are almost empty,
save the rain and a few dark figures,
heads bowed,
shoulders hunched to try to keep out the cold wetness
on their necks and down their collars.
A few people still not ready to call it a night,
to go home to their spouse/children/dog/nothing/no one.
These souls will not see the
amazing beauty of the huge moon.
They never look up.

DAWN

All this pain and all this fighting,
nothing going right,
no one seems to get my vision,
nobody can see my light.
I reach for the sun
and it takes far too long,
I can't catch it yet,
I can't see the bright song
that I know is coming,
I can feel it
if I breathe and dream on.

Dawn will come,
close your eyes,
when you least expect it,
it will arise.
Dawn won't be hard now
so be still somehow.
Trust in the darkness
and know it will pass,
this limbo won't last,
because dawn will come.

I've been hunting forever
wanting to feel
that feeling I get when
I turn the wheel,
when I know I'm in charge
of my life and my deal,
when this paralyzed
feeling will finally heal.
It shouldn't be this hard,

open up your heart,
love with all you have,
play to your own melody,
whisper while you lay,
and dream your fears away.
Trust your chance is here,
because now the Dawn is clear.
Dawn will always come.

HOW BEAUTIFUL

It took three years
for me to be freed
of the ropes and the chains,
of all my own defenses,
my own ways to fight myself.

The rooms were refurbished
and still so the same,
I forgot how beautiful they were.
I forgot how much joy there was,
I had only thought of the pain.
The bad times were the last memories,
but the good times were the more.

The kitchen felt so warm tonight,
the stairs and our old room,
and I waved good-bye and walked outside.
But through my tears I saw
how it really was,
how it really could be,
and I felt my rage pass out of me.
My last defense was gone at last.
My heart was wide open
and love poured in.

LISTEN

The everglades are so still,
like snow in winter storm.
Press on, press on, press on,
my dear girl, are you sure you're warm?
Have a seat and listen for a bit.

The cocoa is hot
and here's a plate of scones.
Buck up now, tough girl,
nourish yourself first.
Easier to do for others what you cannot do for you.
Love requires you be still
and listen to your heart talk;
it will say all it feels
and all it wants.

Come on now, dear girl,
know you are safe today,
know you are safe forever
in this living forest of green.

The falling trees are all an illusion;
when you open your eyes again
the everglades will be standing strong.
Pick up, pick up your chin,
strong girl,
the scones are growing stale.

LAY DOWN EASY

I've been crying all summer wondering why you're gone.
Everything was so perfect
until you told me you were done.
You said she wanted you back,
she begged you come right now
to her house, and to her bed,
and baby I just don't know how
you gave it all away
so fast, in the blink of an eye,
in the tick of just one heartbeat,
without even taking breath to cry,
because I loved you for all time,
because I wanted you as mine.

Baby, lay me down easy,
don't stop to talk,
no pretty pictures of us,
please run don't walk,
I can't bear the thoughts
I've got running round in my head
of you and her together,
her dress undone, her lips of red,
so lay me down easy, baby,
and go fast instead.

I've been crying in my bedroom
wishing you would call
and tell me this is all a nightmare,
that you're halfway down the hall
coming by to see me, to wrap me in
your arms,
she really just meant nothing,

it was all a foolish charm.
I gave you all of me,
I opened up my heart,
so why does she seem
better in your eyes,
why'd we have to part?

First day of September and
I wake up with the Sun,
I haven't seen it in a while,
with my shades all drawn.
I open up the window
and forget to check the phone,
for the first time since
you left to make sure
there's still a dial tone.
You're still with her, see,
but I'm just fine,
everyone's got an open window
and you're no longer mine.
So I'm sending you a box with
the rest of all your things,
this way I can lay you down easy, baby,
so there's no longer any strings.

LAST LESSONS

I'm working hard to stay strong,
I'm trying to be brave,
but life's lessons work me so hard,
sometimes I just collapse.

Taking a risk on love,
can be the hardest thing to do,
it takes everything you have,
to open your heart again.
But risks are worth the heartache,
because between a bell and a bottle,
it's not that hard to rearrange.

Give me the power of separation,
and the strength to hold on tight,
the will of my expression,
and the courage to sometimes fight.
It's hard to find the middle
of the strong and then the weak,
one is lost without the other,
that's the last lesson to keep.

MY WAY

When Daddy showed me
the keys to the car,
he said this is how near,
he said this is how far.
He then tried to warn me
of the rules of the road,
the way that he saw them,
his own stop and go.

Don't merge without checking first the side door,
when you're less than half full, just stop for more,
never go wrong down a one-way,
and please, baby, please, kneel down to pray,
and take your time every day.
But I did as he did, not as he say.
I was losing my way.

But my eyes lit up
when I saw the keys,
there in my hand,
to do as I please,
I waved as I pulled out
as fast as I could
and I tried not to cry—
he never was good at doing good-bye.
When I hit New Orleans,
I pulled up to a bar,
I laughed and said yes
when they opened the door.
And I heard Daddy's warnings
as I downed my first drink,
but I couldn't erase the empty

beers in our sink,
and Daddy's empty seat next to me in church –
and the glasses go clink.
The boy I hung out with through the whole Mardi Gras,
asked me to take him
for a ride in my car.
Well, Daddy'd been down this road,
that's how he lost his way.
So I opened the car door
knowing just what he'd say.
And as we peeled down the highway, the boy leaned in to
kiss me,
kiss me away,
and I saw it all clear as day:
I was merging without checking first the side door,
I was less than half full but not stopping for more,
yea, I was going wrong down a one-way,
I was losing my way.
So when he leaned in to kiss me, kiss me away,
I knew I was losing my way.
I turned the car around and sent the boy on his way,
And I kneeled down to pray.
I was finding my way.

BELIEVE

It's three am she calls me up
and wakes me from my dream,
I can't go on
my life's a nightmare
and he's no longer here.
I talk her down
and go pick up my pen
to try to write it all down.
Because my journal won't let me down no matter the season.
He makes my world shine these days,
but his binges keep
messing with his moods.
They're no uppers he says with a grin
and I know I'm already too far in to back out.

Believe,
please believe,
in the lights and the dreams
and the upside of life,
in the sun and the stars shining on you tonight,
please believe.
Life is a highway
of exits and off ramps,
if you see what you want then go get it.
Life may not come around again
right away, so don't forget why you came here.

Five am and I'm finally ready to sleep
when the doorbell rings
and he's standing there with a smile,
come outside, I've got something to show you.
No, it's late and I turn to go back

but he grabs my hand, please
don't shut the door on us.
If I only knew how to say no
to my heart and the feeling I get
when I want him,
so bad I can't sleep for days if I don't
give in.
It's so hard to turn back when you're lonely,
stretched thin.
Don't fidget, don't shout,
but do let it all out,
he whispers in my ear in his backseat.
She never gave up,
she just wanted a sign,
something that she could believe in.

FLY

Aiming for high
but not catching the air,
raising the bar
but it seems no one cares.

You've got some nerve
the way you treat me,
bringing me down,
a case of bad gravity.

The weather it's turned,
too chilly for shorts,
cold to the bone,
but it can't numb the hurts.

I'm floating on empty,
but I can't fill up,
surrounded by falseness,
let the truth wake us up.

Remedy this,
and remedy that,
you can't judge a book,
when you're face down on the mat.
The skies are clear
and no storms in sight, so...

Fly,
spread your wings and fly.

A set of black hearts,
don't mask the pain,

like a pair of reds
can outlast the rain.
Feelings they matter
it's not just your will,
and the harder you push,
the less you can stop me...still.

You show up big,
and you speak up loud,
wanting attention,
needing a crowd.
I feel myself walking,
walking away,
waving good-bye to
the slap on the face.

Remedy this,
and remedy that,
no storms in sight, so...
fly.

I AM HERE

The ocean waves roll in,
I'm left alone to body surf,
the wetness covers me,
the salt caresses my skin.

I ride a wave to shore,
the sun lights up my face,
a little voice inside me speaks.
The voice is too loud to ignore.
It's my voice. Not yours.
And I am here, hearing something.

MOMENT OF HEALING

I wanted to run
I wanted to hide.
My mind was racing
and life was overbearing.

I stood on the porch
and took one breath
a long inhale and
then exhaled.
And I felt more like myself.

Stay in the present
and don't look back.
Don't get stuck
and go off-track.
The moment of healing
is in the now.

In this moment,
it's all okay.
It's today.
Not yesterday.

The moment of healing
is right here, right now.

LOVE SURVIVES

She waded about,
wanting the starfish but reaching for nothing.
She was a step too late, a step too slow;
she was scared of surviving.
The pail in her hand was red,
the handle white.
It banged on her knee as she waded.
As she waded alone,
she fought to stay by the shore,
for the water was stronger than she.
She looked, her head bent to the ground,
no longer sure of what she was wanting.
The pail brushed the water, she
reached her hand in
and felt the cold wetness and squealed.
Her soul woke up from feeling nothing.
And as she felt the waves caress her skin,
she knew she was strong enough to survive anything.
Free and no longer weighed down by grief,
the sea showed her survival.
The waves collide.
They break and glide.
And love survives.

ACKNOWLEDGMENTS

Thank you to you — the readers — for going on this journey with me. May you find comfort in your healing and courage in yourself as you step forward through your loss.

To my husband for the endless support of my poetry.

To my children for inspiring me every day.

And to Daddy — here's the poetry collection I promised you I'd publish one day. Thank you for sharing a love of poetry with me.

ABOUT THE AUTHOR

Autumn Rae writes inspirational poetry in a contemporary style. She writes many of her poems late at night while the rest of her house is sleeping.

When she's not writing, Autumn Rae loves to travel and hang out with her husband, children, and kitty, who runs the house.

To receive an email when Autumn releases a new book, sign up for her newsletter!

www.autumnraeauthor.com

www.ingramcontent.com/pod-product-compliance
Lightning Source LLC
LaVergne TN
LVHW021411080426
835508LV00020B/2554